A TIGER'S TALE

By

Beryl A. New, Ed.D.

A Handbook for Educators Who Want to Build Relationships with Their Most Challenging Students

Beryl A. New, Ed.D.

Beryl A. New

ISBN:0692268669
ISBN-13: 978-0-692-26866-7

DEDICATION

This book is dedicated to every committed educator who has answered the call to raise <u>all</u> of the children in our village by building authentic relationships with them and their families.

This book is also dedicated to the memory of Rick "Tiger" Dowdell, a student who just wanted someone to listen. May his death not be in vain. Thank you, Tiger, for your inspiration!

Who were your schoolhouse heroes when you were growing up?
The lady in the cafeteria who gave you extra milk? The bus driver
who always greeted you with a smile when you boarded the bus each
day? The teacher who let you wash down the chalkboard or clap the
dust from the erasers?

Do you remember your high school principal's name? Was he or she
more than a mythical personality who you did not know personally,
but did see from time to time? If you had a problem in high school,
who did you go to for help?

Can you identify your principal as a strong personal supporter in your
high school?

If not, is that why you entered this calling?

Would your students and staff identify you as a strong presence in
their school <u>and</u> their lives?

If so, or even if not, this book is for you!

***

"Your dreams are the windows to your goals.

Beryl A. New

CONTENTS

All students need to feel valued. All students need to know that someone with authority is willing to listen to them. Equity is critical, but it is up to the student to decide whether or not he or she wants to access it. School leaders cannot be dictatorial. School leaders must be approachable. School leaders must build relationships with students and their families. Students of color are especially sensitive to issues of perceived unfairness. The insincere "benevolent principal" is offensive to students of color and their families. Vestiges of frugally-doled and monitored services hearken students of color and their families back to semblances of slavery. Students of color and their families know their rights. When rights seem to be withheld, students of color and their families may protest. Unanswered protests lead to revolt. Public revolts stimulate sympathy. A sympathetic public will side with the underdog. Unreasonable insensitivity can damage the career of a well-meaning school leader.

These are truths that I have learned in both my research and in my professional experience. My doctoral dissertation entitled, <u>A Fire in the Sky: Student Activism in Topeka, Kansas and Lawrence, Kansas High Schools in 1969 and 1970</u>, (2007) highlighted pivotal events that occurred in three public high schools just because students felt that their administration did not "hear" their concerns. These students felt ignored, disrespected, insignificant, and marginalized. I know their frustrations firsthand, because I was one of them.

For more than a quarter century, I have worked with high school youth and their families as a teacher, a counselor, and an administrator. I have served the poorest of the poor and the wealthiest of the wealthy. A common denominator among these students has been their basic need to be heard and known – validated. In his research relating to what motivates humans, Abraham Maslow ranked safety just above our <u>basic</u> physiological needs, those needs we have in common with animals. Included in the area of <u>safety</u> was security in both familial and social situations; students need to feel safe at home and at school. The next level higher was <u>love</u> and the knowledge of belonging among friends and family. Then <u>esteem</u>, which included being respected by others, experiencing confidence, having respect for others, and having potential for achievement. Needs within these four levels were categorized as "deficiency needs". When these needs are not met, any human will experience insecurities and stressors. Within an academic setting, these two factors can predict the difference between success and failure. They can also trigger angry responses which will lead to self-harm or harm to others. A number of school-based acts of violence have stemmed from students feeling detached from the mainstream and ignored by adults. If students are to be able to work well and learn, it is imperative that those who create and monitor the learning environment are addressing all students' needs on these levels.

How do school leaders meet these needs? By cultivating a relationship with every student. The process costs little more than your time and commitment to develop authentic relationships with students. *Know every student by name.* Or, at least know every student by face. *Do your research.* Check the progress status of at least 80% of your students each week. *Greet students by name daily* in the hallways, lunch room, and classrooms. *Communicate strongly to students that you are their advocate.* *Practice your role as a supporter* who works from the bottom up. *Assume that parents want you to develop a positive relationship with them,* no matter their socio-economic status. *Remind yourself daily that respect is foundational, critical, and essential.*

"How can I do all this and still get all my management duties done? Besides, what is more important – being in the hallway talking to students, or keeping the central office off my back?"

I'm so glad you asked!

ACKNOWLEDGEMENT

I ACKNOWLEDGE THE GREATEST TEACHER AND LEADER WHO EVER LIVED, WHO ONE DAY ASKED FOLLOWERS THIS QUESTION AS THEY WERE ON THEIR MISSION TO SAVE THE WORLD:

"WHERE IS YOUR FAITH?"

Today, I ask you the same question. Do you believe in your potential to help every single student on your class roster or in your school building to achieve success? Do you believe that every single student who enters your schoolhouse doors has the potential within themselves to be successful at learning and in life? Do you believe that you were called to this profession for a purpose? Do you believe in your own potential to succeed in this calling?

If you don't, you have two choices: either read this book and become inspired, or close it now and begin job-hunting; either way, you will be giving your students the greatest gift of all – a chance to enjoy an abundant life, full of fulfilling learning experiences!

Cracking the Shell

"Tiger is Dead"

Relationship-building is a critical skill for educators like you and me who want to become proficient in the best practices for developing positive behaviors, critical thought patterns, and self-confidence in teenagers – especially those who attend schools in America's urban areas.

Youth in 400 B.C. were much like their counterparts of the sixties, seventies, and today. Socrates, reputed to be a youth magnet, accused his students of tyrannizing their teachers. Yet, he likely died for encouraging many of them to question the accepted norms, to challenge their parents, to think for themselves, and to change practices that were ineffective, insensitive, and nonsensical.

Aristotle reflected, "The roots of education are bitter, but the fruit is sweet." At the root of changing unfair educational practices in the Kansas communities of Topeka and Lawrence is the story of young Mr. Ricky "Tiger" Dowdell. Ricky was a militant at Lawrence High School during part of the 1969-1970 school year. Yet, he was brilliant. He was a leader. He was mature and politically-savvy. He was a visionary and an activist. He was shot in the back while demanding and negotiating changes in the local public high school and university systems.

His is a story which must be heard by all educational leaders if we are going to be impacted by the importance of listening and responding appropriately to students' concerns. It is apparent that "Tiger" knew, as did Sophocles and other great thinkers, that "[a] city which belongs to just one man is no true city." Like Socrates', Tiger's life was sacrificed in order to produce the fruit of inclusion that students in these communities enjoy today. That sacrifice cannot be in vain. It will not, if we truly learn the moral of his tale.

The name "Tiger" denotes one who is powerful, like the large jungle cat. Personality characteristics associated with this name are pointedness, sharpness, strong independence, and high levels of creativity with drive and ambition to have experiences and

11

accomplish things out of the ordinary. People given this name, or nickname, may be destined to experience obstacles to their progress or restrictions on their freedom to act; potentially creating a sense of frustration which leads to feelings of resentment, rebellion, and intolerance. However, people called "Tiger" may also have a clever, quick, and capable mind; but their progress in life may be restricted by instability in their affairs and misunderstandings with other people. Their impulsive nature can lead them to taking actions which they may regret; or may lead to them meeting accidents.

These attributes accurately describe a young man whose story haunted me from the moment I discovered it. I was introduced to Tiger while completing research for my dissertation, A Fire in the Sky (2007). Tiger and I were students in high school at the same time; but, we never met each other. I was attending Topeka High School, while Tiger was a student at Lawrence High School. Our school communities, only thirty miles apart, were experiencing the same levels of student unrest at the same time due to the absence of authentic communication, rapport, and social respect between students of color and school administrators. At both schools there were few, if any, Black students represented on student government committees, in school royalty selections, or on the cheer squads. Both schools' curricula lacked racial diversity, with no Black history or literature courses offered for students to select as required or elective classes. Teaching staff at both schools had few Blacks on the faculty. When parents and students in each community would question the disproportionality in representation, they were either ignored or pacified with promises of a "look" into the issue. That "look" did not occur until students at Topeka High and Lawrence High staged dramatic demonstrations and walked out.

Topeka High School, where I was a participant in the Black student walkout, did not experience any property damage; but my classmates and I did remain out of school for about two weeks until the Board of Education finally responded to our manifesto demanding change and implemented policy that would ensure those changes would be a permanent part of district procedures.

Changes did not occur quite as quickly or as peacefully at Lawrence High School. A group of students, mobilized by Tiger and other young radical leaders, also orchestrated a walkout. However, these students broke windows at the school and started fires following a large riotous fight between Black and White students. Many of the students were injured. The police department dispatched officers to remain at the school and in the area for days. Black students were frustrated because they had submitted to the principal a manifesto outlining the changes that needed to take place at the school and had requested an appointment to visit with him, along with their parents. White students had ridiculed their requests and bombarded them with racial slurs.

Nearly all of the Black students in the school participated in the walkout. Those who may have missed the notice to appear were rounded from their classrooms by their peers. Teachers who tried to prevent participation were disregarded and some minor confrontations occurred. These actions finally aroused a response from school staff and district administrators. The superintendent and school board helped to arrange an evening meeting in the auditorium for parents, teachers, students, school leaders, and community members to review the issues and attempt to resolve them. Tiger was slated to be one of the primary presenters. That did not occur, though. So, following the evening meeting, the bulletin board in the school was set on fire, windows were broken in the school, and the Administration Building next door to the high school suffered a fire bomb attack. An arrest warrant was later issued for Tiger and John Spearman, Jr. (former honor student at Lawrence High School and then-president of the KU Black Student Union) related to the damage that was done to the school. Both were eventually arrested for coming into Lawrence High School and willfully disturbing the peace, but they were quickly released on bond.

The mayor and the governor instituted a curfew to quell the

unrest that was spilling over into downtown Lawrence from both the high school and the university. The imposition of a curfew did not end the unrest, though. In fact, Tiger's execution by a Lawrence police officer rapidly intensified the racial tension that had been growing for more than three years.

You see, three years before his death, perhaps when he was around the age of fifteen or sixteen, Tiger had addressed the members of the Lawrence Human Relations Commission about how Black youth in Lawrence were treated by the Lawrence police officers. Mr. John Spearman, a strong supporter of the Black students and the father of John Spearman, Jr., as well as the only Black member of the Lawrence school board, described Tiger as "...a bitter, frustrated young black kid" in his 1970 interview with journalist Bill Moyers (1972). Yet, he also shared with Moyers his admiration for Tiger's commitment to challenging the community to change the way they treated Blacks. He also admired Tiger and his brothers for their drive to complete high school in spite of their near-orphan status and undeserved focus of blame for every criminal act that took place in the city.

Tiger was a tall young man, six-foot-five, according to Dick Raney, the owner of Raney's Drug Store. Mr. Raney also described Tiger as a dependable, hard worker who had consistently done a commendable job for him. Tiger was not fearful. Rather, he was a calculating champion for social and civil rights. He had done what needed to be done in order to raise awareness about the plight of the high school students. Yet, he had a bigger responsibility facing him. He was a key participant in activities that were taking place at the same time on the campus of the University of Kansas. His intellect and motivational skills had won him a respectable status among young college militants, and he spent a lot of time on the university campus. But, he was also loved and acknowledged as a hero by many of his high school peers. Raney's own daughter, Michelle, wrote him a brief, emotional message about her former schoolmate on the night

14

she heard the news of his death. Raney shared her cryptic words with Moyers. "Tiger Dowdell is dead."

Like Tiger, John Spearman's own son had also navigated this racist school system; but John, Jr. had been taught by his parents that he was as good and as smart as any other student. He had performed very successfully in high school and won a number of awards and academic accolades. Yet, beneath his surface compliance festered anger so intense that it would drive him to orchestrate destruction at the institution that well-prepared him for academic success and leadership, the University of Kansas.

Even without strong parental guidance and school supports, it was evident that Tiger was also intelligent and eloquent, performing well beyond his years as a leader among his peers and older university students. He was a planner of political protest rallies, a change agent for fairness and justice, and a brilliant strategist for facilitating these changes. How could such a gifted intellectual have been overlooked by his high school teachers? Rather than nurture his gifts and celebrate the outcomes, as school staff routinely did for White students, school administrators and city officials sought ways to entrap, cage, and finally destroy the "Tiger".

On July 16, 1970 at around 10:15 p.m., police officers raided the "Afro House" near the KU campus where two men had allegedly passed through the house following the shootings of at least two area residents. Tiger, thought to be one of them, reportedly ran in the front door and then fled out the back door, possibly calculating his options for survival to fight another day. Twenty-seven year old police officer William Garrett chased him down the alley, then shot and killed him. Garrett claimed self-defense; however, one eyewitness stated that she did not see Tiger with a weapon before he ended up face down in the alley with a gunshot wound in his head.

Moyers chronicled his conversations with Black and White Lawrence residents in the days surrounding Tiger's death during a cross-country tour entitled, Listening to America (1972). He had stopped in Lawrence at the invitation of the city's newspaper publisher for what he anticipated would be a brief respite in a quaint Midwestern town. He happened to be in Lawrence on the day that Tiger was killed and was able to interview a number of residents, both Black and White, about the reasons leading up to this pivotal event. He concluded his chapter on Lawrence with findings published in the <u>The Report of the President's Commission on Campus Unrest</u> (1970). They reported that there was "an incredible lack of communication" in Lawrence among Black and White citizens. This disconnect had led to decades of horrific levels of death and destruction, the most tragic being Tiger Dowdell's.

How many "Tigers" walk the hallways of our schools? Do they strut, or do they crouch? Are they predators, or simply trying to meet their basic needs to survive? Are they discounted, suspended, or expelled because we see them as a threat? Are we fearful to have a warm and genuine encounter with them? Tiger was a visionary, a leader, a martyr, a lesson in communication and justice, and sadly a young man for his times but yet before his time. Tiger was a fighter who laid down his life for a cause. Tiger had the potential to become a Black American hero. But, Tiger was marginalized, hunted down, and finally destroyed by those who had the ability and multiple opportunities to embrace and nurture him. Tiger's is a tale that should not be forgotten by educational professionals who are willing to celebrate the unique passion and beauty of the "Tigers" in our schools.

Had Dr. John Ogbu, noted cultural anthropologist and Univ. of California, Berkeley professor, met Tiger, he likely would have categorized him as a "disenfranchised" student. Tiger was a young man who developed what Ogbu (1991) termed an "oppositional cultural identity" by internalizing this perceived discrimination. He made many attempts to talk with those who had the power to solve his and others' problems, but they were not willing to listen. Both city and school leaders had given him a deaf ear for more than three years. His demonstration, then, moved from speech to action. Ogbu would tell us that when dealing with disenfranchised students, their rebellion may often be demonstrated in their clothing, their music, and their speech, including angry rap lyrics, graffiti, racial slurs, and cursing.

As long as societies evolve and new ideas emerge, students will have a reason to protest. The administrators who have the responsibility of modeling the process of beneficial interchanges within an academic system must learn to listen to students' concerns and cooperatively work toward resolutions. It is apparent that protesting students just want to be heard. Students will care about schools that care about them. When students' racial and emotional needs are satisfied, they are prepared to learn and their capacity to learn is increased.

From his research, Eric Schaps (2005) reflects that a caring, supportive school environment positively affects students' academic success, including their attitudes, motivation, engagement, goal-setting, desire to stay in school, drive toward graduation, grades, and assessment scores. As founder of the Developmental Studies Center in Oakland, California, Schaps has dedicated years of study to understanding more about the academic, social, and emotional development of young learners. His research has demonstrated that more youth are likely to develop positive attitudes about themselves and pro-social attitudes and behaviors toward others when they can learn in a positive, responsive environment. Students who may have any number of reasons to be angry at the world can demonstrate positive behaviors when they enter a school that is caring and supportive. In confirmation of this fact and based on his own years of scholarly work, noted educator and innovative program developer Dr. James Comer (1996) writes, "No significant learning occurs outside of a significant relationship."

In his Handbook of Competence and Motivation, Edward L. Deci and collaborators (2005) confirmed that when the sense of community is low, especially for students of color and low-income students, they may be placed at further disadvantage by the quality of their experience in school and therefore lack "a sense of belonging". Deci has done extensive work on developing the "self-determination theory", which examines factors that motivate humans to make certain choices. He writes that when schools fail to meet students' need for belonging, the students become less motivated, more alienated, and poorer performers.

Recently, a random group of students at my school were interviewed by an outside implementation coach. These were the responses they candidly shared with him:

"Teachers work with you before and after school...if teachers didn't take the time out to help me, I wouldn't have stayed in school and been on track to graduate...every day they inspire kids but they don't know it...teachers listen to you and you can talk about anything...it feels like family...Dr. New is like our grandmother...administrators are cool, approachable, and know your name...we are not the 'ghetto school' everyone thought we were...no racial tensions – very integrated...everyone has a bond with someone..."

We have intentionally worked very hard to make sure no "Tigers" can hide in our school. We won't let them be ignored, even when they try. Whether they attempt to cloak their needs underneath a black trench coat or a scowling demeanor, we recognize that they just want to be heard and then find ways to convince them that we are willing to listen.

***

"Unfinished business kills every investment."

"Can We Talk?"

There is a story told about an African village where all the newborns were mysteriously dying. After a few months of this tragically reoccurring, the doctors in that area called in a group of researchers to help them assess why the mortality rate was abnormally high all of a sudden. At the conclusion of their research, the experts called the hospital staff in to report their findings. When they shared the information, all of the doctors and staff members began to respond in an angry denial. Some were insulting and even disrespectful toward the research experts.

You see, the researchers had told them that they – the hospital staff – were responsible for the hundreds of deaths! The hospital practice had recently changed to schedule operations in the morning and birth deliveries in the afternoon. But, when the morning surgeries were complete, the physicians and their attendants had done a poor job of washing their hands before going in to deliver the newborns, and bacteria and negligent hygiene infected the infants and led to their deaths.

As difficult as this is to imagine, it happens symbolically in our classrooms and schools every day. It appears that adults who have been entrusted with the responsibility of delivering our youth to adulthood and success don't care enough to clean up our situational environments to the point where they can be nurturing, protective places for our young people to mature in a healthy way. Many in our society don't want to invest time, effort, attention, or money into creating youth success stories; but we will pay taxes that go toward supporting incarcerated teens at a price tag of more than $25,000 a year. Sad to say, my Midwest state's crime rate is above the national average, and a growing percentage of those criminals are youth.

So, what about the children? Who, if anyone, cares? We ourselves believe, and certainly want others to believe, that we entered the field of education to make a difference in children's lives. I personally promote the maxim that there are no throw-away children, none who deserve to fall through the cracks, none who should be left behind. I would not want any of those things to happen to my own children, and I am committed to ensure that none of those things happen to any child in my professional care. We are committed to raising our students' hopes for future success, to raising their expectations of themselves, to raising their spirits through our encouragement and support, to raising their self-esteem through our words of affirmation and committed actions, and to raising them to become adults who will raise their children well. This is how the village will become stronger and grow healthy. It takes all of us to raise the village, and it takes the village to raise the child.

When I was old enough to think about a profession, I thought I wanted to be a nurse. However, when I got to high school, I decided I wanted to be a psychologist. In spite of all the nurturing, encouraging teachers I encountered from elementary school to high school – Mrs. Baker in first grade who allowed me to shine each day as I read aloud to the other students; Mrs. North in third grade who instilled in me pride in my penmanship; Mrs. Counts in fourth grade who taught me the most wonderful classical songs; Mr. Tidwell in fifth grade who helped me refine my social skills; Mr. Wetlaufer, my junior high principal who loved every kid he met; and Mrs. Welty, my high school English teacher who inspired my love of the English language and all of its intricate mechanics – I also encountered an uncaring, disconnected, disingenuous counselor in high school who not only did not know me, but also did not care enough about me to review with me my own post-high school goals. Instead, she counseled me to not plan to go to college because I was not college material. She recommended that I enroll in secretarial school. I blindly followed her referral, even though it was not based on a relationship or even a smidgen of knowledge about my skills and interests, because she had never taken an opportunity to ask. Later, though, I followed my own dreams and enrolled in our local university, where I completed both my bachelor and master's degrees in education and graduated with high honors at both levels.

I became a teacher because I loved English. Then, I became an educational leader because I loved serving students. At each level of advancement, I have been able to help more students, clearing their way to success in school and in life while making the conscious decision to operate as a servant leader, not a leader over servants. "What is the difference?" one might ask. The answer is as obvious as the difference between a paycheck and a passion.

The decision to <u>serve</u> as an educator is a personal one. You have to determine for yourself the level and amount of responsibility you are willing to invest into taking care of the children and raising the children. Where would you be today had someone not valued you as a child, as a young person, or even as an adult? Can you afford to not also pass that care and concern on to other children – not just your own but also all of those in the village?

The art of passing on the traditions and values of the village is not one just left to the elders. How will we know our practices will be continued unless we train the next generation to replicate the good things we have learned to do? I find daily that compassion rests in some of the most unlikely breasts. Not all victims seek to become victimizers themselves. Many have transformed from victim to "victor", and are eager to be the champions for justice and equity.

Never make the assumption that poverty equates to insensitivity. I have witnessed many examples of students who lack the most resources being the first to share whenever the opportunity arises. Maybe not so surprisingly, these same students are also bright high achievers. There is a correlation between the practice of protective and compassionate instincts and a positive feeling about oneself. James Rilling and Gregory Berns (2002) have researched this phenomenon. When we help others, the brain becomes stimulated in areas that turn on the same responses as when we receive rewards or experience pleasure. Young people who demonstrate this practice get the same pleasure as they would if they were gratifying a personal desire.

When we create caring school environments, not only do we

lessen the likelihood of violent incidents, but we also teach our young people a way to feel good intrinsically. Might those feelings replace a need to create an artificial euphoria through drug abuse or other negative routes to self-gratification?

"But, you don't know my kids!" you might argue. "They've had no home training. Their parents don't care. They only come to school because the judge told them he would lock them up for truancy. They have no goals. They're just here to terrorize teachers and intimidate their classmates." Oh, really? How do you know for sure? Maybe through their demonstrated behaviors; but, have you talked with them individually? Do you care enough to ask them about their goals and dreams? Do you make time to help them get on track to achieve those goals?

A sixteen-year-old Hispanic male at my school was the identified "general" of his gang. Though small in frame, his followers were extremely loyal and he "ran" many individuals who were much older than him in the community. I didn't care. I wasn't intimidated by him. I would smile at him and send him and his buddies on to class if they dallied in the hallway within a few seconds of the tardy bell.

I had to call him in to visit with him on two occasions. One was when we found graffiti on the wall in one of the men's restrooms. He was seen on surveillance camera leaving the restroom close to the time the graffiti was reported. How did I know it was him? We only had three incidents of graffiti in a two-year period and one was to mourn the death of a former student. The other two related to two different gangs attempting to mark their territory.

What all of these budding artists later found out was that this was actually my territory; and just like they would not want me to come into their home and start drawing on their bedroom wall, I wasn't going to tolerate them doing the same to my walls. Those three students agreed with me on that point. Once we got that understanding and they had to scrub down the toilet wall and everything around it, we had no more incidents of graffiti. It's funny how a little elbow grease mixed with logical accountability goes a long way!

The second conversation I had with him centered around him being tardy multiple days within a week's period. When I called him into my office to talk with him about that, he shared that people came from Mexico and stayed at his house. They brought their children with them, and his mother had to drop them all off at school before she dropped him off. I suggested to him that she drop him off first, since high school started before grade school. He looked at me very seriously and then repeated that he had to be dropped off last. I could see he wasn't going to budge on that point, but I still emphasized to him how important it was for him to be on time for school. He smiled and said that he would try.

I found out later that, due to his high level of authority in his gang, he was expected to supervise his mother in making sure the children of the visiting, higher-ranking gang leaders were delivered to school. That was his job, and being on time for school himself was inconsequential. I knew I needed to pursue a different line of attack. So, I brought him in for another conversation. By now, we were enjoying our visits with one another! This time, he shared some of his mainstream goals. He wanted to be, surprisingly, a police officer or a fireman. The first time he mentioned this, he looked at me as if he anticipated my disbelief. I kept my face straight and told him I thought that was great! We talked about some community mentors who had experience in both of these areas. I set him up to shadow a local police officer and gave him information about the junior officer training.

He still maintained his gang role, but he brought none of the activity to the school. He began going to class and doing well. He would let our community liaison casually know about anything that may have occurred in the community after hours or over the weekend so that the liaison could have a heads-up to visit with key players and eliminate gang issues within the building.

Things were going well until one Valentine's Day. I had been out of the building for a district-level meeting. When I returned, my secretary looked distressed. He had been looking for me all afternoon! I thought, "Oh, no! I wonder what happened!" Before I could question her about what he may have told her, she smiled and pointed to a Valentine he had left for me. Surprise! That could not have happened with that student in this community or within this school without relationship!

The good news is that he went on to finish high school. He knew that I and others had high expectations for him in spite of the influences of his family and lifestyle. Therefore, he adopted high expectations for himself. There is a positive correlation between an educator's spoken positive expectations and a student's performance. You may be familiar with the work of Robert Rosenthal and Lenore Jacobsen, and James Rhem's (1999) citings of their work, related to the Pygmalion Effect. Students will live up to teachers' expectations for intellectual growth and performance, or live down to their lack of expectation for their growth and performance. Progress in either area is commensurate to the level, high or low, of expected performance communicated by the adult.

I could have fussed at him about his choices, his lifestyle, his lateness, and his affiliations. I could have told him he would never amount to anything if he continued down that path. Those words would have been grounded in truth, but may not have had a positive effect on his performance. Instead, I connected with his stated goals and assured him that he had the potential to be successful. Then, I referred him to mentors who could guide him on his spoken journey. He had hope in himself because adults verbally affirmed their hope in him.

This is why relationship-building is critical for student survival. His was a family that existed below the poverty level. He was likely doing what he knew he had to do as the only man in his household in order to keep a roof over their heads and help his mother and siblings survive in a non-native land. These are not optimum, nor ordinary, circumstances; but, this was his reality. Could I leave him where he was and say, "Oh, well…" No! Neither should you. There is no child in your building that you can afford to ignore. Every child in your building is worth saving.

***

"Like a spider's web, what you build comes from inside of you; then, it supports you, attracts what you need, and gets you to where you need to be."

Meet Me at the Corner

"What Do We Do In Common?"

As educational leaders, we operate within a professional creed. We believe that all children can learn. We believe that every child deserves access to a free and appropriate public education. We believe that education is a civil right. We believe that our students and their parents deserve highly qualified professionals delivering a challenging curriculum in every classroom. We believe that our future lies in the hearts and minds of the youth we educate. We believe that we have been called to serve every student, no matter their culture, color, or creed.

A challenge to some educators occurs when we are confronted with the "Tigers" in our school. These students often look out of place. They may hide their true potential in order to fit in with certain groups. They may have been discouraged as early as the second or third grade when an insensitive teacher attempted to control their aggressive intelligence with a seat in the corner. Sometimes, these students – usually males of color – were inequitably disciplined. Some of them were targeted for special services placement and treated as if they had learning disabilities; when actually, they may have been the brightest and most inquisitive student in the classroom. Some were ignored, stifling their willingness to participate constructively in the learning process. Many were systematically turned from excited, energetic, playful cubs into stealthy, mistrustful, predatory "Tigers". How could we have allowed this to happen?

Think about your own child's early learning experiences, or that of a relative or friend. Would you have tolerated a teacher who strongly communicated to the child that they were not welcome in his or her classroom? Would you have tolerated a principal who ignored your concerns and supported this teacher's discriminatory behaviors? Of course not. Have you heard these horror stories, though, about other teachers and principals? Have you shared conversations with frustrated parents who have lost faith in the educational system for these reasons? Are you aware that gross inequities exist in how students of color have historically been treated in public education systems?

These are prime conditions for creating the jungles in which our "Tigers" learn to survive. They are mandated by law to attend school until at least the age of sixteen. We are mandated by professional responsibility, however, to make school a place that will welcome and nurture every student. There are, though, things that the law cannot force us to do. Being accommodating, welcoming, nonjudgmental, and impartial are some of those things. Our own heart's conviction must legislate our own actions.

One factor that impacts this professional responsibility is the phenomenon of racial responsibility. How does it play out? You see a child misbehaving in the grocery store and her mother has a very harried look on her face. So, you smile at the child and say, "Come on now, Sweetie. Aren't you the nicest little person? I <u>know</u> you're a good child for your mother!" Mom gives you an appreciative smile, and the child looks at you like a cat looking at a new piece of furniture. In that brief distracting interchange, you have interrupted an emerging tantrum and the mother has regained her sense of control. In the village, this is what many elders will do to strengthen the family.

It did not matter that these were not people you personally knew. There was a communication of expectation from the elder to the child for improved behavior, as well as a concern for the well-being of the mother and the child. This expectation was acknowledged on both sides. It may or may not have been because you were of the same color. It was likely because the implied expectation of good behavior was strongly communicated, and the child responded.

Have you ever been driving down the street and seen two elementary school children fighting? I have. What did you do? Did you stop your vehicle, roll down your window, and shout at them to stop (like I did), stating that their mother was going to get them for fighting? (I didn't know their mothers, either – to my knowledge – but the threat worked!) Did you drive more slowly and give them the "I'm watching you" look? Did you laugh and keep on driving? Or, did you barely glance and then ignore them? How you responded may have been determined by your personal commitment to the good of the village.

There is a natural tendency for animals and humans to care for those who look like them. Humans develop affinity with other humans on a variety of levels; but commonly on facial appearance. They connect with individuals who may not be known relatives or friends, but simply share the same skin color. Humans may also demonstrate stereotypical reactions to humans who don't share their skin color.

How many times have you struck up a familial conversation with someone you have never met before and discussed a number of common topics due to a relationship based solely on your comfort due to sharing the same skin color with that person? Someone you are with may ask, "How do you know them?" You reply, with a chuckle, "I don't!"

How many times have you shown favoritism to someone of your own color "just because"? How many times have you cheered for an unfamiliar team or voted for a candidate just because that person had the same color as you? Consciously or unconsciously, humans find themselves in these situations throughout their daily life. Often, the only explanation for their support of an individual, or lack thereof, is skin color.

Humans may also be more highly sensitized to injustices done toward people of their same skin color. Crimes committed by someone of one race upon someone of a different race can rouse anger and frustration simply based on knowing that the victim shared your same skin color. Blind support for an issue that is drawn on racial lines occurs often, as evidenced by blogger comments around news stories.

Couched in humor but steeped in real-life concerns, these comments reflect perceptions that often emerge within conversations among racial groups about movie plots: "Why does the Black guy who always gets killed off first in the horror movie?" "Why does the White guy always have to be the villain?" "Why does the White girl always have to be the victim?" "How come the Mexican guy is the one who has to be the drug dealer?" "Why do the Asians always have to own the businesses?" Of course, none of these generalities <u>always</u> exist, but they have been expressed often enough to make individuals question the patterns.

Valid concerns arise when these urban myths drive practices in social, political, and public settings. In a school, the goal is to educate all children equitably and without prejudice. If you are an educator in an urban setting, you may have heard colleagues who share your color make statements such as, "I don't care. I'm looking out for <u>our</u> kids!" "If Black kids have any trouble with these White teachers, they need to let me know. <u>I'll</u> take care of them!" (Or, vice-versa.) This becomes a sad commentary on the way educational leaders allow their staff to conduct their daily business. Every educator should be focused on providing the best education possible to <u>every</u> student, no matter what color they may be. However, behaviors such as the ones illustrated above reinforce the phenomenon of selective racial responsibility. If we are to lead effective schools, these practices cannot be allowed to exist, as they will often weigh out over professional responsibility.

The danger in ignoring this potential powder keg in schools is the fact that it serves to further disengage our "Tigers". They are consistently on the alert for signs of discrimination, preferential treatment of others, and inequities. When these issues occur within a racial scope, that is often all they need to go into survival mode, release their claws, and start to tear things up. We cannot afford to let this happen, for their sakes and for others.

Relationship-building is critical for student survival.

Relationship-building is also critical for administrator and staff survival. One key issue which emerged strongly from the walkouts at the high schools was lack of relationship and communication among students of color and their school leaders.

The call to teach is a gift. There is a level of dogged commitment that comes with answering that call. As much gratification as we receive from seeing the light bulbs come on in our students' minds or seeing them cross the graduation stage to celebrate their success, we also receive the grief of a fault-finding public or a disappointed family. It is not easy to take the bitter with the sweet. However, we are the cooks. We plan the menus. We can decide what we serve because it is good and healthy, and what we throw away because it's rotten or potentially harmful.

We share common expectations for our students. We know that reading acquisition is critical to lifelong success. We believe that strong math skills are the gatekeepers to higher educational pursuits. We know that soft social skills will take a student far in the professional world. We wouldn't settle for less for our own children.

Students who live in poverty experience a unique set of struggles in these curricular and social areas. Just because a family may live within a low income range, it does not necessarily mean that their children will be low performers. Certain factors ensure school success. Among those are parents reading to their children on a consistent basis, high expectations for school success and appropriate classroom behaviors by parents, and the ability for parents to navigate in-school services for their children. When any one of these factors are absent, especially in families at or below the poverty level, educational success is compromised.

Children whose parents read to them from infancy and even into early school years develop early reading skills and continue to be capable readers throughout their lives. When their parents or their older siblings teach them to read, they develop a desire to continue to read. They also increase their vocabulary at an age when language acquisition and retention is expanded.

Children whose parents do not read to them early, or at all, often enter school at a deficit. Public pre-school programs may attempt to bring them up to school readiness-level within a year or two, but it seems that once this lag exists, it is perpetuated even throughout high school. Once the gap between students who had a positive start and those who did not exists in reading and math comprehension, it is very difficult to close fully.

There is a direct correlation between low income and low reading scores, but the root of our students' issues in these areas may have something more to do with community deprivation and the generational failures of public schools within those communities. If a student's parents were not challenged to be successful in public school but were ignored and discounted, they likely did not have a good school experience. Therefore, if they did not experience success and instead built a history of negative or even traumatic memories, they sometimes hesitate to return to these institutions themselves, even to advocate for their child. They may also communicate to their child an attitude of mistrust for the institution and its leaders, continuing this cycle of self-perpetuated destruction. This is often how we breed the "Tigers" within our schools.

In 2011, according to data published by the Annie E. Casey Foundation (2013), nearly 75% of the fourth graders who scored at the low end of the National Assessment of Educational Progress were from low-income families. This assessment measured third grade reading proficiency. These same children were slated more four times more likely to drop out of school before earning a high school diploma than their classmates reading at a proficient level.

Many students also experience the double-whammy of low reading and low math skills. However, we also have a number of "Tigers" who, like Tiger Dowdell, are brilliant thinkers, writers, and speakers, yet struggle with mathematical concepts. Those at my school who had this issue were interviewed individually. Of the thirty-nine we talked with, only two said they also were not strong in

Language Arts. The others all said they liked English and Social Studies and did well in both courses. However, they got discouraged and gave up on math because it was too hard to understand how to make numbers and letters make sense when they were combined. We hired a teacher who could work with these right-brain learners and explain the formulas to them in a way that they would understand; and by the end of the semester, ninety percent of them successfully completed the Algebra course that they were failing during the first quarter of school.

It is scary to imagine how limited their possibilities would have been had they not been able to pass this entry-level math course. When these capable students do not experience success in math, they find ways to avoid taking a math class altogether. When they realize the inevitable and enroll in the most basic level available, their options related to career choices are greatly reduced. Right now, our country needs our students to be trained in science, math, and technology. But, the higher the level of math anxiety, the more likely a student is to avoid math classes, math tasks, and math careers. Researcher R. Hembree (1990) has conducted a number of studies related to test and coursework anxiety. His findings determined that there is an "undeniable relationship" between math anxiety and math avoidance.

Armed with this knowledge, we have a responsibility to respond. May our "Tigers" be "growling" because they are frustrated with themselves, not angry with us? May this be their way of communicating a need and an expectation that we will provide them with some answers? Would a simple conversation start the process toward total school success for them, eliminating the barriers between us and them as well?

We ascribe to the education of the "whole child". This suggests that we are committed to meeting their intellectual, emotional, spiritual, physical, and social needs. We must therefore continue to maintain a "front-and-center" focus on the hidden needs of our children. There are issues they want us to discover in them, just as there are qualities they yearn for us to praise. This is why we have been charged with this mission – and if we are willing to partner with them in this task, we will find that we can do it successfully!

***

"Everyone deserves your respect; especially you."

"All in Your Face!"

Accountability. It's a loaded word. It suggests that I know what you are supposed to be doing, and I am going to make sure you do it. But, what about myself? It is often easy for us to look at others and make determinations about our expectations for them, given their position and outlined responsibilities. But, how about what we think when we look at ourselves? When we challenge that person in the mirror, are we saying things like, "I'm doing the best I can." "People don't understand how complex my job really is." "I wish I was back at the beginning of my career when every day was a joy. Now, it's just a job."

Personal accountability requires a high level of self-reflection. That can sometimes be uncomfortable for people who feel that they are presently giving all they have and have no other resources from which to draw. For them, it may be easy to make excuses or compare themselves to others. The challenge becomes moving from their current functioning level to a greater level of effectiveness and productivity.

"Tigers" can bring out the worst or the best in you. You're having a bad day. The superintendent entered your building just as a parent was leaving, cussing you out for suspending their child. What else could you have done? He set a fire in the handicapped restroom! The cafeteria staff got wiped out by a flu virus, so you need to hurry over there and make sure lunch is ready for the students. Before you can head for the cafeteria, though, a staff member marches "Tiger" into your office, glares at you, and says, "Do something with him!"

Pause for a moment. What will you say to the staff member? What will you say to Tiger? This is a prime opportunity for reflective problem-solving. Have you ever taken a course of action with a student that you later regretted because you acted out of frustration? Did you place undue blame on a staff member for dumping her classroom management issues in your lap? Who benefitted most from your decision – you, the staff member, or Tiger?

Throughout my career, I have made it a priority to be student-focused first. Adults can always come second. However, students know that I will consistently follow the school policy and if they violate a rule they will receive the corresponding discipline. But, life in the jungle is not usually black and white. Many factors may determine Tiger's actions, the teacher's response, and my evaluation of the situation.

In spite of the beauty and diversity found in the jungle, dangers are teeming everywhere. Predators, quagmires, disease-carrying insects, stealthy attackers – all exist for their own survival and others' destruction. Possibly in their own minds, they do not see themselves in any sort of negative light. They are just trying to live another day. However, to those on whom they could inflict serious harm they are seen as a nuisance or a danger, and their goal becomes one of elimination.

Unfortunately, many of the "Tigers" in our schools are seen as nuisances who should be eliminated. They may make staff uncomfortable because of their quiet, sullen demeanor. They haven't done anything – yet – but they can't be trusted. They just might go off one day. However, many of these on the elimination list should probably be placed on the endangered list – Black and Latino males whose external characteristics mirror music video "thugs" in dress, tattoos, hair styles, and speech. Again, these are the "disenfranchised" students that Dr. Ogbu (1991) urges us to engage so that we can see their beauty shine. They are gifted artists, musicians, writers, and deliverers of the spoken word. Many are fascinated with science and history. Many can quote facts and trivia that would make them "Jeopardy" game show champions. But, many go under-appreciated because they look like "Tigers".

Predators help keep the jungle balanced so that no one species dominates the others. Quagmires sweep the jungle floor of debris and maintain a healthy ecological waste system. Disease-carrying insects also help build immunity against epidemics which could wipe out a large number of humans. Stealthy attackers show mercy in not setting up a state of panic among many when they just choose their one target that will ensure their survival. These functions are all necessary for the cycle of jungle life to continue. Everyone has a role, and if they each fulfill their individual responsibilities the environment remains productive for all.

In the case study outlined above, who plays each role? Both educators and students may be the monitoring predators. Each one looks out for the interest of themselves and their group, but a balance in communication and collaboration must exist for the environment to remain healthy. Like the quagmire, administrators should constantly assess the school's system to ensure that outdated, ineffective, and unfair practices are discontinued so that new and current practices can flourish. The stab of truth can often sting like a jungle insect's bite, but it brings about positive change and growth. This is a step in the process of improvement that we cannot avoid or choose to ignore. As leaders who are wise and stealthy as a jungle predator, we must exercise "super" vision at all times. We have to see what is coming and be proactive about addressing change. We cannot afford to bury our heads in the sand of ignorance. If an issue needs to be addressed, we must learn to do it in such a way that the individual is addressed rather than the group. If one teacher continually dumps her minor discipline issues in the principal's office, the plan for growth should not be addressed in a general staff meeting with all of the other staff who do their part in building relationships with students and avoiding classroom disruptions through good class management, but with her in private consultation.

So, how would you handle Tiger in this situation? Does he need a good fussing out, or a big hug? Maybe both. However, he will accept neither from anyone with whom he does not have a relationship. It is evident that the teacher lacks that level of collegiality with Tiger. If she did, he would likely not be in your office with a request for you to "do something". Prior conversation would have clued her in to what he needed at that moment, and she would likely have engaged you as a facilitator toward meeting his need, if she believed the need was something she could not handle herself.

Let's assume that, even though she had no real working relationship with him, you did. Could you sit beside him and allow him to explain what happened in the classroom from his perspective? Could you listen without interrupting him and making hasty judgments? Could you let him know how you would support him if he can only conclude that she was having a bad day and taking it out on him? Or, if he had violated a classroom or school rule, could you review the policy with him and let him know that he would serve the appropriate penalty, but you expected him to respond differently in the future? And, could you do all of this as he walked with you to the cafeteria and helped you to organize lunch for all of his fellow students?

How do you think Tiger would have felt about school after this experience? What could you do to follow up with the teacher so that she will have a supportive reception ready for him when he returns to her class? Remember, she is the highly qualified professional in the classroom and expected to demonstrate mature judgment and professional behavior at all times. She may have been extremely stressed at the moment, but tomorrow is a new day and a fresh start for everyone. If Tiger is expected to do that, she must model it. He will feel validated as a human being and know that we all have our shortcomings, but we work together to maintain balance in the jungle.

Blackboard Jungle (1955) is a movie in which Glenn Ford stars as a high school teacher and Sidney Poitier is a student he engages into school simply by developing a relationship with him. At the beginning, Ford, Mr. Dadier, is very distrustful of the large sullen Poitier, Gregory Miller. In fact, Mr. Dadier suspects Miller of all types of subtle, destructive acts. But, he takes time to get to know Greg. When he does, he finds out that Greg is a very talented musician and singer and had a great mind. Mr. Dadier begins to plan his instruction around topics and activities that are current and relevant to his students. They stop misbehaving in class and begin to enjoy the discussions and the teacher. In the beginning of the movie, Miller told Mr. Dadier that he was going to drop out of school at the end of that school year. At the end, he leaves telling Mr. Dadier, "See you next year!"

In social history, this movie is heralded for being the spark which started the youth rebellion. The song, "Rock Around the Clock" was the hallmark for the Rock and Roll Movement in America and England. It is interesting to note that the movie also addressed the issue of disengaged and angry students, such as Tiger, and the lengths they would go to in order to get the attention they craved from adults in their schools.

The true villain in the movie was not the large, intimidating Black student – Gregory. Instead, it was the small, subversive White student, Artie. In fact, Artie was so diabolical that he prank-called Mr. Dadier's wife to such a terrifying degree that their son was born prematurely. He survived, but Artie did not survive the jungle. He ended up challenging Mr. Dadier to a fight in the classroom and was escorted from the school in handcuffs. Who built a relationship with him? He was the delinquent who sat in the back of the room and cried out for negative attention. But, he still managed to be overlooked until he caused a potential problem by pulling a knife on the teacher in the classroom.

Some may conjecture that he escaped early discipline because he was White. People always expect the Black kid to create the problems. Hopefully, that is not true; but to some students, it seems that way. Disproportionate suspension data for Black and Latino students in comparison to White students committing the same acts bears out the truth in this conjecture. Yet, educators cannot allow themselves to get caught up in the color game. It is impossible to undo three centuries of wrongs to people of color. No human alive today is three hundred years old, so no human can assign nor accept blame for what happened in that shameful era. But, it is possible to begin where you are right now and assess whether you are color blind or color struck. Both are debilitating when it comes to building relationships.

Color is a necessary part of our world. Colors define beauty and also danger in nature. Colors add diversity and variation. Color is superficial, though. It provides little more than a differentiation in tone. In humans, it is a measure of the amount of pigment in the skin. But, color does not identify intellect, nor does it describe character. It adds variety, but not value. To become color blind would mean the loss of appreciation for all of the beauty that exists in the world because of color. Blindness indicates loss of sight. Yet, to be color struck would mean an undue fixation on the perceived value of color. If you're light, you're alright. If you're brown, we'll let you stick around. But, if you're black, you'd better get back! To be color struck indicates a level of blindness to humanity that can be dangerous. When we value ourselves or our students based on something as superficial as skin color, we have lost the opportunity to see the real value of us and them as individuals. Our challenge is to educate our staff and our students on the importance of appreciating our differences, not judging each other on the basis of them.

***

"Relationships are like flowers. The more you cultivate them, the more they grow."

When I Grow Up...

"Common Goal-Setting"

Every human, whether we admit it or not, wants to feel appreciated and noticed. The Tigers in our schools and our lives need to recognize that we value their diversity and their skills, and they need this validation more than most of us know. What else do they need?

- **Stability of resources.** When Tiger arrives in my classroom each day, he is looking for the familiar and the comfortable. It must consistently be present for him to thrive and trust me.

- **At least one advocate within the system.** When Tiger can't talk to anyone due to his own frustrations, he needs to know that he can go to a place <u>and</u> a person for a cool-down period and be listened to when he is ready to unload his fears and frustrations.

- **A challenging curriculum.** Our Tigers are not stupid or slow. They are generally quick thinkers who have already come to the conclusion that certain staff won't believe that they are intelligent and capable students. Their minds have to be challenged by teachers who are confident that they can be successful.

- **Consistent encouragement toward success.** Our Tigers can spot a fake adult a mile away; and by the time they encounter them, that fake is fresh meat. But, they also thrive on opportunities to focus on their goals and be encouraged by their genuine cheerleaders along their journey.

- **Nonjudgmental interactions.** So what if you don't know Tiger, have never met him, and have no relationship investment in him? He still needs for you to approach him with an authentic smile and an open attitude. He is used to the suspicious glance and the nervous smile. Those hurt his spirit, though. What he and every other young person values is the adult who sees <u>them</u>, not what they have on or what color they are.

In order to build productive relationships with our students, we need to know about them. We need to know the things that they and their parents are willing to share with us, and we need to know the data embedded in their stories. How are they performing in their core content classes? How many tardies and unexcused absences have they accumulated? What services might they or their families need? Are they on track to graduate from their level with their cohorts?

For these answers, we must gather data – the hands-on way. The following steps will help you develop a plan to support at-risk students.

1. Make a list of your targeted at-risk students. Leave no one off of the list who could benefit from support in order to be successful in school and demonstrate improved behaviors.
2. Select your criteria: test scores, attendance data, behavior incidents, and graduation-ready status.
3. Meet first with both parents and students to outline the interventions they identify and those supports you and your school will provide.
4. Schedule regular meetings with the individual student. Review past assessment scores, past performance grades, and the last time the student felt successful in school. It may have been in the primary grades of elementary school, but it is important to begin by identifying the components of the student's school experience that made him most happy and optimistic about attending school.
5. Have available at the first meeting at least one piece of data that demonstrates that student's potential. Make sure they look at it and affirm that it is an area of strength for them. This will be the new springboard for their success.

6. SPEAK POSITIVELY OF THEIR SUCCESSFUL OUTCOME. Make sure they can also verbalize their potential to be successful. Numerous studies confirm that positive affirmations can change the trajectory of an individual's movement from negative to positive outcomes.

7. Partner with support services within your building. Either introduce the student to another supportive adult who you believe will be a good match for the student, or ask the student to identify another staff member with whom they share a positive relationship. The goal is to widen the student's scope of supportive adults so that there will be multiple human resources available at all times.

8. In the next meeting with the student, ask him the following questions:

   - What do you want your future to look like?
   - What do you see as your human value?
   - What do you assess as your potential?
   - What are your grades telling us?

   Then, use this information to shape a plan that fits the student specifically and individually.

9. In upcoming and ongoing meetings with the student, complete the following tasks:

   a. Monitor student progress at preset increments (mid-quarter, quarter, and semester).

   b. Have the student chart their success from the beginning to each data gathering point.

   c. Celebrate that success with the student.

   d. Develop an overall performance outcome chart for the student.

   e. Examine the distribution – did he meet his goal? Was he close? Did he demonstrate growth? Did he fail?

f. Target the areas where he failed or nearly failed. Develop a plan of action for his improved progress. Praise him for his effort.

10. Chart the student's individual progress for him and have him update the data during ongoing visits.

11. If you are working with a group of students, use a monitoring document like the sample provided to measure how your efforts are supporting students. Make changes as needed in the plan, and adjust according to the student's growth and need for support.

Many at-risk students operate in survival mode. They may hoard everything from the free snack you hand out to your time. Following are a few areas to watch to ensure that you are not turning into the host for a parasitic Tiger.

✓ Be the At-School Support Person as much as possible. Rides to doctor appointments, hair appointments, grocery store trips every Saturday, personal loans, middle-of-the-night taxi services, etc. all weaken your academic support role. Emergencies do come up, and it is important to help in any way you can. But, make sure that the lines of professional responsibility are not blurred by someone trying to take advantage of you.

✓ Be objective about the student's discipline. If he has done something that warrants a discipline consequence, don't block it because he is your pet project. He will develop an unfair sense of entitlement, which will cripple him in the future. Growth toward success involves learning from your mistakes and making better choices in the future. Don't block his opportunities to learn the principle of cause and effect.

✓ Be mindful of the student's academic schedule. He may need to make some unscheduled visits to you in order to navigate a crisis that may arise from time to time. But, don't allow him to use your office as a hangout to avoid classes. Know that his need is valid, but send him back to class as soon as possible.

Hopefully, we want our students to mature to become self-supportive and independent. We can provide structure, guidance, and targeted supports but we cannot obligate ourselves to carrying them indefinitely. As they practice success and experience success, they will also learn how to create and maintain success. That is when we back up and celebrate their flight. We must resist the urge to over-monitor. That tendency transfers to overkill very quickly.

The work you do with and for the Tigers in your profession bring innumerable results. You will have opportunities to see them emerge from their sullenness into a confidence that only comes with the knowledge that they have something very valuable to add to their world. It is affirming to have just one of them tell you that you have made a difference in their life. But, even if none do tell you that, you must know that you have; and that knowledge is the impetus you need to encourage you to continue to do this difficult but rewarding work.

***

"Don't climb to the top by stepping on people."

AT-RISK STUDENT MONITORING GROUP DATA REPORT

		GOAL	Previous Period 1/21-1/24	This Period 1/27-1/31	Percent Change		YTD
Students Meeting 7 of 7		80%	39.2%	38.5%	-0.7%		--
			282/719	276/716			--
Attendance		95%	85.79%	87.73%	+1.9%		88.38%
On Time Rate (Unique Students)		97%	92.7%	93.4%	+0.8%		95.1%
			421	433			
Discipline	Total	5% Weekly Decrease of Total	39	52	+33.3%		1822
	Other		16	26	+62.5%		1027
	ISS		15	24	+60.0%		682
	OSS		8	2	-75.0%		113

"Reproducible Results"

Many of my presentation engagements have come from professionals hearing me talk about my school and the momentous gains we have made over the past few years. Emerging from the sixth lowest performing school in our state to become the highest performing high school under a federal School Improvement Grant in our state, we have much for which to be grateful.

"How did you do it?" people often ask. I talk about the data driving our decisions, about how important it is to make authentic relationships with students, how instructional staff must be trained in research-based methods for delivering curricula and engaging students, and how technology is key in providing our students with 21st century skills. I share with them dozens of anecdotal stories of individual student successes, as well as outcome data that we accumulate on a daily basis. I stress how important it has been to have our leadership team all on the same page when it comes to expectations for high levels of success across the board. Yet, it is also important that we maintain a balance of diversity so that every base is covered. I describe our model environment – a clean building, orderly classrooms with one focus wall painted a specific color based on brain research, the same select colors chosen for all hallways and the cafeteria to stimulate calmness or thinking or appetites, adults in the hallways to greet students and monitor passing-time activities, and student service offices interspersed throughout the building so that an authority figure is always just a few feet away.

Those factors are just the framework for our success. The heart, blood, and soul of our school family is the relationships we share. Students have transferred from our school to enroll in another district high school. Two months later, they want to come back. Each one of the returnees has shared that no one cared whether they were in class or skipped at the other school, so they came back to us because they knew at least we would fuss at them for not being in class. They said they recognized that we were a family and they missed being part of the family. To me, that is the greatest compliment we could have received.

However, it's not enough to sit around singing, "Kum-ba-ya" and hugging one another if no one is getting a quality education in the process. We must have professional accountability, challenging curriculum, and identifiable boundaries in place to make our school feel safe and secure for our students. But without the heart, blood, and soul of the school, the structure is very cold and unwelcome. A balance must exist.

I cannot tell anyone how to run their building. I am content to "sweep around my own front door." Yet, I can share the factors that have helped students I have worked with become successful learners, and perhaps those ideas can inspire someone else to try something different, or perhaps affirm what they are already doing.

I share with my staff at the beginning of each school year that we have the joy of supporting students, not the other way around. None of us would be employed in this field if we did not have students who needed an education and parents who needed our support in that process. Therefore, students come first. I designed a student-centered pyramid to illustrate that concept. At the bottom, you will find the administrative staff. Support on a number of levels comes next, but the student, his family, and the community are at the top. Our responsibility is to assess their needs and then develop our programs to support those needs, not the other way around. Too often, we want to design the programs and then try to squeeze the students and their families into our design. Sadly, our designs have not taken their needs into account, so our events are poorly attended and our efforts are not well-received.

We may find that some educators agree with this model; but, some may not. Power is a dangerous ally in that it is extremely deceptive. It can help us to access what we and others need, but it can also go to our heads and make us believe we have more of it than we actually do have. To have earned successive graduate degrees is commendable. Why did we pursue learning at advanced levels? Was it to feel fulfilled when we see the multiple letters behind our names? Was it to achieve a personal goal? Was it to advance to a level where we could have greater influence over people? Was it to get into a position to help more people?

We are the only ones who can answer that question about ourselves. Hopefully, though, somewhere in our motivation was the goal to help more young people.

AN INTER-DEPENDENT ACADEMIC COMMUNITY'S
STUDENT-CENTERED FUNCTIONAL PYRAMID

⭐ **STUDENT** ⭐

STUDENT ADVISING STAFF
College/Career Counselor, Seminar Teacher, etc.

STUDENT SUPPORT STAFF
Principal, Counselor, Social Worker, CIS Worker, etc.

STUDENT INSTRUCTIONAL STAFF
Teachers, Paras, etc.

DATA/RESEARCH STAFF	CURRICULUM COORDINATOR	INSTRUCTIONAL COACHES	ATHLETICS/ ACTIVITIES COORDINATOR

ASSISTANT PRINCIPAL	ASSOCIATE PRINCIPAL	PRINCIPAL	ASSISTANT PRINCIPAL	DISTRICT LIAISON

As an Academic Center and Community Resource, we are responsible to all of our stakeholders, but especially to our STUDENTS AND THEIR FAMILIES.

I invite you to take the Educational Philosophy Quiz on the next page. Along with that, review the self-survey below. They each may tell you some things about yourself. Be honest with yourself. After you have placed a check mark beside each statement that describes you below, study the sequence of marks. The key to the survey is at the end of the questions.

Self-Survey

1) I think any student can pass a class if they just do their work.
2) I am not concerned about a student liking me; I just want to know that they have learned what I am teaching them.
3) I learn all of my students' names in the first week of school.
4) I take pride in being colorblind and treating all of my students the same.
5) I became a teacher because someone I respect inspired me.
6) It doesn't matter what data says. Kids are kids. Some will pass and some will fail.
7) I think I would be unhappy outside of the field of education.
8) Unless a student decides to be successful, I can't do anything but provide an opportunity.
9) I would like to learn more about new ways to track student progress, but I don't know where to start.
10) We need to shift the focus from a teacher's strategies to a student's attitude.

If you placed a check mark beside a majority of the **odd numbered statements**, *you are <u>primarily</u> student-focused.*

If you placed a check mark beside a majority of the **even-numbered statements**, *you are <u>primarily</u> teacher-/administrator-focused.*

©2014 by Beryl A. New

Educational Philosophy Questionnaire

Please respond to the following questions using a scale of 1-5, with **1=strongly disagree; 2=disagree; 3=neutral; 4=agree; 5=strongly agree**.

	1	2	3	4	5
Every child can learn successfully.	1	2	3	4	5
All kids connect with relevant curricula.	1	2	3	4	5
All kids know who cares and who does not care about them.	1	2	3	4	5
All kids will come to school just to see the people who care.	1	2	3	4	5
Learning can, and should, be fun.	1	2	3	4	5
Learning can, and should, be disciplined.	1	2	3	4	5
Young adults present mental brilliance in a variety of ways.	1	2	3	4	5
All kids respect educators who keep their word.	1	2	3	4	5
All kids respect educators who have high expectations.	1	2	3	4	5
All kids respect adults who model respect toward them.	1	2	3	4	5
All kids will perform the way you expect them to perform.	1	2	3	4	5
The young adult potential is immeasurable.	1	2	3	4	5
All kids need rules and parameters to feel safe.	1	2	3	4	5
There are no throwaway kids.	1	2	3	4	5
All teachers must be willing to be perpetual learners.	1	2	3	4	5
The student is the most important person in the academic plan.	1	2	3	4	5
Teachers who care about a student's success will do anything they can to support it.	1	2	3	4	5
Students demonstrate knowledge and content mastery in many different ways.	1	2	3	4	5
There are no "bad" kids. All of us are individuals, with unique dispositions.	1	2	3	4	5
Knowledge is power. The more knowledge students gain, the more opportunities for personal fulfillment become available to them.	1	2	3	4	5
The student must always be the most important person in the academic plan.	1	2	3	4	5

Where are your highest scores?   ©2014 Beryl A. New

Our most affirming outcome will not only be to see our Tigers emerge as successful learners, but also to see them inspire others to do the same. Success breeds success, and youth listen to their peers. Meta-research analyses have demonstrated that peer teaching yields some of the highest percentages in student learning. Many of our Tigers are leaders within their societies. If they walk left and exit school, ten others may follow. If they can be shown their potential for success by walking right, though, those ten and maybe ten others will also follow. Unfortunately, Tiger Dowdell chose the left path, and it cost him his life. It is up to us to identify our Tigers early and help them to see the alternative so that they can live to lead another day.

***

"We all have two hands. If you use the right one to take good care of yourself and others, you still have the other one left to take care of others and yourself."

BIBLIOGRAPHY

Berman, P. (Producer), & Brooks, R. (Director). (1955). *Blackboard Jungle* (Motion Picture). United States: Metro-Goldwyn-Mayer.

Comer, J. (1996). *Ralllying the whole village: The Comer process for reforming education.* New York: Teachers College Press.

Deci, et.al. (2005). *Handbook of Competence and Motivation.* New York: Guilford Press.

Fiester, L. (2013). *Early warning confirmed: A research update on Third grade reading.* Baltimore: The Annie B. Casey Foundation.

Hembree, R. "The nature, effects, and relief of mathematics anxiety." *Journal for Research in Mathematics Education* 21.1 (1990). Print.

Moyers, B. (1972). *Listening to America: A traveler rediscovers his country.* New York: Dell Publishing.

New, B. (2007). *A fire in the sky: Student activism in Topeka, Kansas and Lawrence, Kansas in 1969 and 1970.* Retrieved from ProQuest Digital Dissertations.

Ogbu, J.U. (1991). *Literacy as praxis: Culture, language, and pedagogy.* Norwood, NJ: Ablex.

Rhem, J. "Pygmalion in the classroom." *National Teaching and Learning Forum* 8.2 (1999). Print.

Rilling, J. et. al. "The compassionate instinct: A neural basis for social cooperation." *Neuron* 35.2 (2002). Print.

Schaps, E. "The role of supportive school environments in promoting academic success." *Getting results: Safe and healthy kids* Update 5 (Chapter 3) (2005). Print.

Teale, W. "Positive environments for learning to read: What studies of early readers tell us." *Language Arts* 11.1 (1978). Print.